Dessert knives and a fork (on tray) c.1830 and a selection of fish knives and forks c.1870–1920.

TABLE KNIVES AND FORKS

Simon Moore

Shire Publications Ltd

CONTENTS

Published in 2006 by Shire Publications Ltd, Cromwell House, Church Street, Princes Risborough, Buckinghamshire HP27 9AA, UK. Website: www.shirebooks.co.uk
Copyright © 1995 by Simon Moore. First published 1995; reprinted 2006. Shire Album 320. ISBN 978 0 7478 0295 2.
Simon Moore is hereby identified as the author of this work in accordance with Section 77 of the Copyright, Designs and Patents Act 1988.

Printed in Great Britain by Ashford Colour Press Ltd, Unit 600, Fareham Reach, Fareham Road, Gosport, Hampshire PO13 0FW.

British Library Cataloguing in Publication Data: Moore, Simon. Table Knives and Forks. – (Shire Albums; No. 320). I. Title II. Series 683.82. ISBN 978-0-7478-0295-2.

ACKNOWLEDGEMENTS
The author expresses his thanks to those who have helped him in the researching of this text and in the collating of the illustrations: Bill Brown, Graham DuHeaume, Claude Blair, Anthony Dove, Anthony Stevenson, David Sier and Jenny Moore, also the British Museum, Victoria and Albert Museum, Museum of London, Stuart Devlin, Messrs Phillips Auctioneers, Longleat House, Canterbury Heritage, Dyson Perrins Museum (Worcester), Cutlers' Company in Hallamshire, Sheffield City Museums, Terry Atkins at the Nelson Museum at Lloyds of London, the Royal Geographical Sociey (London), Musée de la Coutellerie (Thiers), Musée de Condé (Chantilly), the Niedersächsisches Landesmuseum (Hanover), the Koninklijk Museum voor Schone Kunsten (Antwerp) and the Deutsches Klingenmuseum (Solingen).

Cover: *A chronology of eating knives (top to bottom): Roman domestic knife, engraved bone scales, fifth century AD; medieval knife, hafted with dudgeon (rootwood) pierced with hearts, fourteenth century; early Tudor Flemish-style knife with hammer finial and bone scales; mid Tudor knife with bone haft crudely carved as a woman with contemporary headdress, c.1550; sweetmeat fork, the haft of ebony, ivory and wood inlaid with silver wirework, c.1620; pair of wedding knives by Jonas Melcher with silver inlaid and jet-collared hafts, the velvet lined sheath worked with gold wire and seed pearls, c.1625; octagonal-bolstered short knife (possibly for a child), the haft of bone and ivory inset with coral and amber roundels, c.1630; square-tipped knife with haft of stamped brass sheet, c.1660; scimitar-bladed knife with brass ferrule and cap protecting the bone haft carved in light relief with flowers, animals and the inscription 'My love is due to none but you', c.1700; scimitar-bladed knife, with silver octagonal pistol grip haft filled with resin, c.1730; dessert fork with truncated end haft of stamped silver, c.1770; ceramic-hafted dessert knife by Elkington with imported German haft, c.1870; dessert knife with stainless steel blade, bone haft, c.1930; ivory-hafted and close-plated dessert fork in a style of the 1880s that set the trend for most table cutlery for the next 75 years.*

Neolithic flint knife, hafted with wood (courtesy of the British Museum).

KNIVES IN EARLY HISTORY

Although table forks were not accepted in the now familiar trio of table cutlery until the later seventeenth century, knives (and spoons) have a lineage dating back some two million years. The earliest knives are, admittedly, crude lumps of fissile stone, such as flint, chipped to produce an edge for cutting and scraping. Not until the palaeolithic period (500,000–10,000 BC) were actual knife blades fashioned from stone into recognisable shapes. By the neolithic period (5000–2000 BC) stone blades were being polished and some were fitted with crude hafts of wood, moss or hide to protect the user's hand.

The first metal-bladed knives, fashioned first from copper and then from bronze (3000–700 BC), show such an improved design and technology that many features of bronze age knives crop up repeatedly in later centuries. A solid area of metal, the bolster, was fitted to the end of the blade nearest the handle so that the blade would not become stressed during use and

Bolstered bronze knife, hafted with bone (courtesy of the British Museum); bolsterless, tanged, engraved bronze blade (courtesy of Klingenmuseum, Solingen).

Socketed and flat-tanged spear-type bronze knife blades (courtesy of the British Museum).

Iron age knife, hafted with bone (courtesy of the British Museum).

start to bend upwards. A spike of metal, the tang, was also cast as part of the bolster, protruding from it, so that a haft of organic material (wood or bone) could be knocked on to it. After casting, the entire blade was finished by hammering (the beginning of the bladesmith's art) and some were decorated with lines engraved with flint-tipped burins. Many bronze age blades were double-edged and resembled spear points.

The discovery that iron holds an even sharper and more durable edge than copper alloys was made about 2000 BC but

Flat-tanged knife (the tang extends only a short way into the haft), the bronze haft cast as a boar's head (courtesy of the Museum of London).

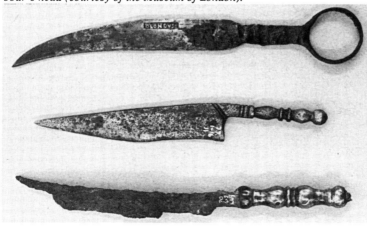

Metal-hafted knives; the blade of the ring-hafted blade has been marked 'OLONDUS' (courtesy of the British Museum).

4

Scale-tanged knife with bone scales and bronze wire loop (courtesy of the British Museum).

Saxon scramasax blade from Sittingbourne, Kent, inlaid with coloured metals (length: 13 inches or 330 mm) (courtesy of the British Museum).

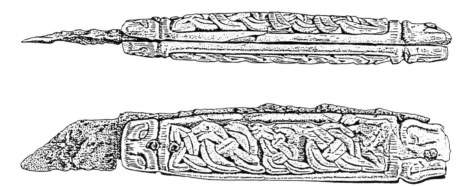

Viking knife with bone haft carved with zoomorphic knotwork panels (courtesy of Canterbury Heritage).

was not used widely in Europe until about 1000–900 BC. Advanced civilisations, such as the Roman Empire, used a great diversity of knives for tasks ranging from eating at table to personal hygiene and the ritual examination of animals' entrails. Roman knives were sophisticated in design and finish; many incorporated a ring finial for easy carrying (which was a bronze age feature). Even more were made with a scale tang, a flat strip of metal pierced with holes for rivets used to attach scales or grips of organic material.

The later Scandinavian and Germanic invaders of Britain brought their knives and weapons, some elaborately decorated with iron age zoomorphs and blades inlaid with coloured metals. There were iron-making forges in some monasteries: writing in the eighth century, the Venerable Bede described how the monks accepted forging iron as a normal duty. Knives were important to everyone: dreadful fines and other punishments were imposed on knife thieves and this most treasured possession, an eating knife, was often interred with its owner.

Evolution of the knife bolster: top, shoulders (c.1500) to small bolsters (c.1550).

THE RISE OF THE CUTLERS' COMPANIES (MEDIEVAL TO MID TUDOR, c.1100–1550)

In most medieval knives the proportion of haft to blade is roughly equal. The blade is longer only if the knife had a special purpose, such as carving.

Both blade and tang were forged from wrought iron as one complete unit. As the art of good and consistent steelmaking was not perfected until the mid sixteenth century, steel was expensive in the middle ages, and so only the cutting edge of a knife was made from steel, being forged on to the lower edge of the blade as a fine-grained strip. Blade tangs were either of the scale type or one of two types of whittle (pointed) tang. The simply made knock-on tang was still the most common even though the through tang which ran the entire length of the haft was more secure; this was either curled around the end or was attached to a metal plate or cap. The knife haft was normally made from horn, bone, wood or a cheap but prettily reticulated rootwood known as 'dudgeon'. Leather was occasionally used for hafting knives with scale tangs since cutlers could buy cheap offcuts from tanners. Ivory was reserved for richer patrons. Each end of a haft was protected by a metal band or collar. Although scale-

tanged knives lacked bolsters a pair of tin or copper alloy 'shoulders' was soldered or riveted on to the blade to separate it from the haft. Swages were ground along the upper edge of some knife blades to increase the piercing power of the point and to act as a partial double edge. Swages are rare on medieval blades.

Late medieval knives were generally scale-tanged and many show Dutch or Flemish influence. These knives are characterised by hafts that terminate in a plaque of copper alloy engraved, with

Opposite: Medieval knife types: c.1100–1500. Note the difference in blade form at this time and the variation in the types of point. Several hafts have been decorated by turning them on pole lathes; several show a reticulated wood which is dudgeon. (Upper row) The earlier blades have been inlaid with coloured metals (c.1100–1200); the knife at far left has been hafted with ivory, a rare material at the time; note the knives with protruding through tangs (c.1200–1400). (Lower row) Most have shoulders at the junction to the haft; several have ring finials to attach to a belt; the knife at far right has been hafted with wood and copper alloy engraved with the all-seeing eye of God and an acorn finial – this may have been used by a freemason.

varying degrees of skill, with human faces and figures. The obverse side often shows a human half figure, usually St Barbara (patron saint of gunners) or St Lawrence (patron saint of cutlers and ironsmiths); the reverse side was normally engraved with animals or just a tangle of lines. Later examples (*c*.1500) were made with copper alloy finials – a horse's hoof, an animal's head, a hammer or a cylinder – and were engraved with zigzag lines to give the effect of chiaroscuro. Many show traces of having been tinned and have been found around Billingsgate, London, suggesting the presence of a Flemish or Dutch cutler or brassworker there.

Sheaths were best for carrying knives but, for those who could not afford them,

the knife's haft was pierced for a cord worn around the waist. Each sheath was cut from leather, decorated with hot stamping irons and waxed; many were given lids, especially trousses (sheaths which held several pieces), which were made either for hunters or to hold carving knives. At noble banquets men of status acted as carvers and presided at the head table. A carving trousse usually contained two richly hafted and large broad-bladed carving knives, the lord's eating knives and a sharpening steel. Carving became an art and in 1508 Wynkyn de Worde published *The Boke of Kervynge*, which laid out the correct terminology and method for carving meat from many types of animal carcass. The pantler, second to

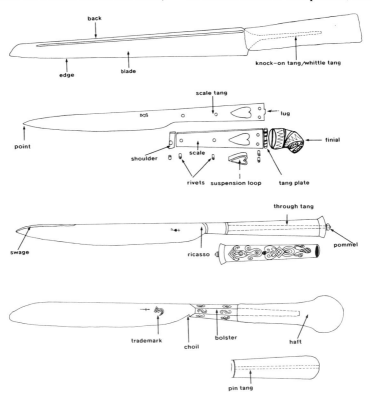

Anatomy diagrams of four knives (from top): c.1200; c.1520, also showing horse's hoof finial; c.1590; c.1640; inset of haft of late nineteenth-century knife.

8

the carver, supplied several types of bread, each carved with a different knife: the mensal knife was used to remove the fine crust of a loaf to present to the lord to show the fine quality of the bread, possibly giving rise to the expression 'upper crust'! Guests were expected to bring their own knives, which they used to cut off pieces of meat. Table courtesy was considered important and Chaucer, in his *Canterbury Tales*, eulogised the exemplary behaviour of the prioress Madame Eglantyne.

Forks were used either to assist in carving or to eat sticky sweetmeats: a will dated 1463 bequeathed to 'Davn John Kertelynge a silvir forke for grene gygoʳ'.

Such delicacies came to be eaten off small wooden platters, known as roundels.

Records of the London Cutlers' Company have been traced back to the twelfth century. In London, knife and weapon blades were produced by the subsidiary 'mystery' of bladesmiths. Cutlers purchased the blades, assembled the knives and sold them together with sheaths purchased from the sheathers' guild; they were ultimately responsible for the quality of each knife and stamped a trademark on to the blade. Substandard wares were seized and offending cutlers fined by the Company court. During the late medieval period there was a fashion for inlaying

Sweetmeat forks and candied fruit: left, c.1400; centre c.1580; right c.1630.

the trademark with coloured metal so that it would show up as the ferrous blade darkened with use.

The Sheffield cutlers were not welcome in London and they were often accused of

Application of steel cutting edges (arrowed): c.1450, along lower edge of blade; c.1580; and c.1930, whole cutting part of blade.

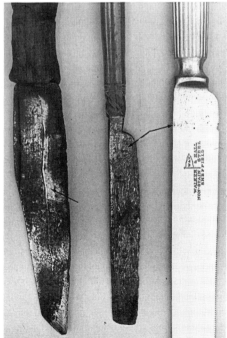

selling substandard and *forreyn* (not of London origin) wares in the capital. Other cutlers from provincial guilds such as Salisbury, Thaxted and Birmingham also tried to imitate the London wares in the hope of better sales. Indeed the Sheffield cutlers were not permitted to form themselves into a recognised company until 1624.

As steelmaking improved, the cutting part of a knife blade was made entirely from steel and by the mid sixteenth century this had become the norm. The bolster and tang were die-forged as one unit in a special mould and then forged on to the steel part of the blade. The join can often be detected as a flush of brighter metal surrounding the blade, forming a characteristic 'puddle' or 'thumb print' – a technique that has continued into the twentieth century. Knife shoulders were also made of iron as an integral part of the blade and tang but were gradually replaced by a bronze age style solid bolster of metal; this led to longer blades and the grinding of swages near the point. Another bronze age feature, the choil, a small indentation of the blade's edge adjacent to the bolster, prevented the bolster from becoming scratched when the blade was sharpened. The ricasso of English knives was left plain; some continental knives, especially from Germany, have been damascened in this area.

10

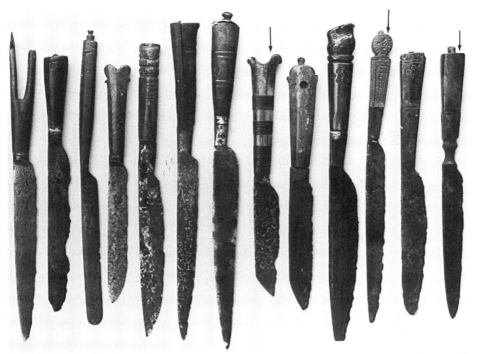

Elizabethan solid-bolstered knives: hafts with tang pommels, brass spacers, use of ivory (arrowed).

ELIZABETHAN AND EARLY STUART
(c.1550–1650)

During Elizabeth I's reign cutlers produced knives of unsurpassed beauty and elegance. Even utilitarian knives were better balanced and more pleasing to the eye; the cutler's art was reaching its zenith as England prospered.

By the mid sixteenth century English knife styles had diversified from those of the rest of Europe as cutlers developed an individuality in craftsmanship and design. They may have been encouraged by the introduction of the continental custom of giving pairs of knives at special occasions, such as at a wedding. Courtiers of Henry VIII apparently introduced this charming idea and so, from the early sixteenth century onwards, the custom of giving 'wedding knives', as they became known, was fashionable in all social spheres. Wearing neck ruffs must have inconvenienced many diners; Louis XIV coped by using a long-handled fork but English diarists seem to have recorded little or nothing of this problem. Tudor portraits show families dining wearing small ruffs and an increase in the length of knife blades may have helped.

Knives were often made in pairs, one to be kept clean and dry, for cutting bread, the other to cut meat and lift food to the mouth. Forks continued to be used for eating sticky sweetmeats and even in the mid seventeenth century this use continued; they usually had a spoon bowl at the other end and this is known as a sucket spoon (Moore, 1987). Fine-quality knives, known as 'Sunday knives', were made to be worn at religious festivals with black ebony hafts for Lent, white ivory or mother-of-pearl for Easter and a piebald combination of the two for Pentecost.

Later Elizabethan knives (c.1580) were made with long sharp-pointed blades, frequently swaged. The blade edge curved

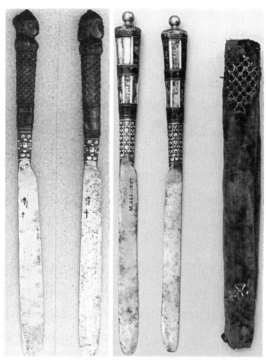

Inset scale knives figured prominently among the everyday knives: the overall design is robust with the steel blade attached to a haft of iron with short scales riveted into the middle part. Finer knives were made longer and narrower, often with octagonal bolsters that were usually inlaid with silver piping, flowers, masks and pellets or gold damascening and set with collars of ivory, amber, jet, agate, rock crystal, aventurine glass, even precious stones. Ivory hafts were frequently left plain, although some were carved into human figures, and a set of fourteen

Another use for the knife point (fifteenth-century Flemish tapestry) (courtesy of Musée de la Coutellerie, Thiers): scallop-shell toothpick with its ivory knife haft c.1580.

outwards almost hemispherically, the back remained straight and the reintroduced solid bolster entered its own experimental phase and was made in a variety of shapes: square, rectangular, polymorphic, cylindrical, all with many variations. For finer knives the tang ran the entire length of the haft, capped either with a copper alloy plate or a small spherical pommel of latten or pewter. Suitably shaped hafts were produced, consistent with overall balance and line. Hafts for square-bolstered knives were often made in a partitioned format with spacers of latten between wider spacers of dark wood, sometimes contrasted with paler-coloured bone and ivory. The hafters' skills matched those of the cutlers: ivory and bone were engraved with swirling designs surrounding roundels of polished amber or wood; many hafts were carved or engraved with inscriptions, sometimes crudely, and with figures of men and women dressed in their finery.

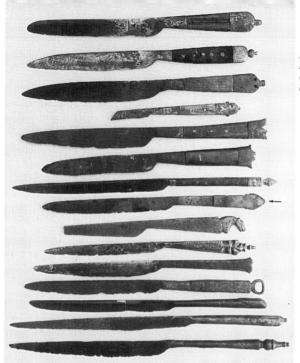

Inset scale knives (top eight) and more slender all-iron knives, c.1550–1600; the arrowed knife belongs to both categories.

Long bolster combined with short haft knives (top three); the remainder show examples of damascening, silver inlaying and haft engraving c.1600–50.

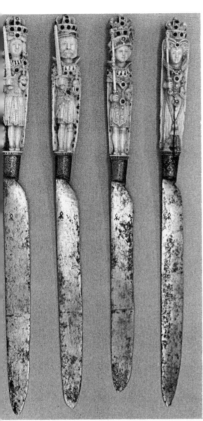

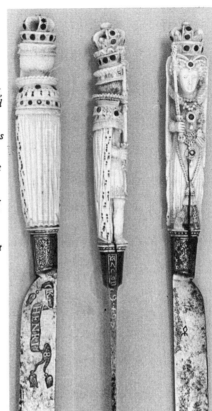

knives, dated 1607, in the Victoria and Albert Museum, London, is hafted with ivory depicting the sovereigns of England from William I to Elizabeth I.

Prices were regulated by the Cutlers' Company and 'A pair of rich knives damascened for the Queen on a City visit' cost the Company 30 shillings. The Company continued to scrutinise quality although a few knives, inlaid with tin or a brassy copper alloy to represent silver and gold, managed to escape their net.

As knives became finer with elaborate hafts and bolsters, the sheathers made sure that they were not outshone. A typical sheath for fine knives comprised single or twin wooden tubes covered with embroidered silk and cloth of gold, worked with precious metal wire, and even stitched with seed pearls (see cover). To accompany the daily costume or a best set of clothes each sheath was attached by a string of rich material. Women presented with such gifts would have felt socially elevated since there was a strong element of snobbery amongst the merchant classes in the wearing of such fine knives. Few period portraits, however, show ladies wearing their knives, although Shakespeare, writing in 1597, insisted that Juliet should wear her wedding knives and the margin of Speed's 1626 map of Europe shows European women in national costume wearing such knives.

The pommels of through-tang knives were replaced by fancy silver filigree balloons or detachable toothpicks as scallop-shell finials, which presumably helped to obviate more vulgar methods of toothpicking! Hardstone hafts were protected by scalloped bands of silver (ferrules) at either end. Despite this decorative precaution many have been cracked and chipped. Amber continued to be favoured as a hafting material, its golden translucency enhanced by underlaying with gold leaf engraved with figures, names and dates of donation. Silver was only occasionally used as a hafting material, although many knife hafts in English collections were made and finely engraved with amazing skill following designs by the Flemish De Bry family.

Simpler knives would have predominated, however, hafted with metal, ivory, cheaper bone and wood, and shaped like a club or cylinder. This type of haft has often been associated with the Commonwealth period when fancy and luxury items were disfavoured. Bolsters were shortened to a 'button' of metal at this time – barely enough to reinforce the blade's fulcrum.

In 1606 the London Cutlers successfully petitioned for a quality control which enforced provincial (foreign) cutlers working in London to strike their wares with an upright dagger mark – a charge in the City's arms – in addition to their own personal trademark. Many London cutlers decided that the dagger represented London and that only they should use this mark! The ruling was reversed but not until 1664, by which time the dagger mark was being used by both London and 'foreign' cutlers. Some London cutlers became famous for their high-quality wares: Peter Spitzer (unicorn head) and Joseph Surburt (lower-case y), who were both foreigners, the Jencks family (thistle), Jonas Melcher (dolphin), Thomas Eament (acorn), John Arnold (fire tongs) and

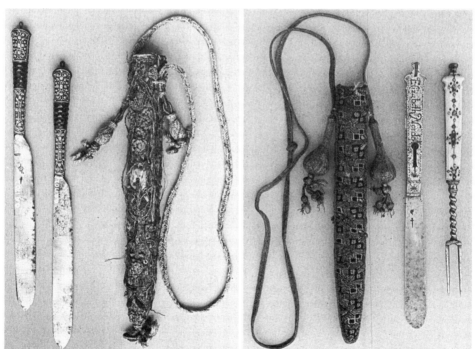

Left: *Wedding knives by the Jencks family, c.1620, the hafts of silver-inlaid iron with faceted jet collars; the sheath of gold wire and embroidery is rather dilapidated. (Courtesy of the British Museum.)*
Right: *Rare slotted (known as 'splay'd') pair of knife and fork by Adam Piggott, presented to Elizabeth Norden c.1670 with wire tasselled and embroidery sheath. (Private collection.)*

15

EИG: WOMAN

Left: *Panel of John Speed's 'European Atlas', 1626, depicting an English woman wearing her purse and knives together. (Courtesy of the Royal Geographical Society.)*

Right: *Pair of agate-hafted knives, probably by John Wessell c.1640; sheath with woven cover; close-up of haft showing detail of silver filigree balloon pommel.*

Above: *Pair of Flemish knives c.1600, hafted with silver engraved with allegorical figures in the manner of the De Bry family; wirework and leather sheath. (Courtesy of Messrs Phillips, Fine Art Auctioneers.)*

Left: *William Brooke, tenth Earl of Cobham, and his family at table, by Hans Eworth, 1567. Note the small neck ruffs. (Courtesy of Longleat House.)*

Designs in silver and niello by Michel Le Blon (courtesy of the Victoria and Albert Museum). (Centre) A knife haft c.1630.

Henry King (snake around a standing cross). Much of the Jencks family's work was of the finest quality and still exists, through careful keeping, mainly in the form of superlative wedding knives.

Although the Sheffield cutlers' company was not granted its charter until 1624, Leader (1905) states that before 1565 some men and women who plied a cutlery trade in the Midlands or North of England had settled in Sheffield since the early medieval period. Hey (1990) suggests that the Sheffield cutlery trade, at this time, was more of a growing industry than Leader implies and has recorded the existence of a Sheffield knife in the King's possession at the Tower of London as early as *c.*1340, fifty years before Chaucer wrote about a Sheffield 'Thwitel' in the *Canterbury Tales*. He also records John Leland's observation (*c.*1505) that 'Ther be many good smithes and cuttelars in Halamshire' (L. Smith, 1964). The Sheffield cutlers made good use of the water power in the area to drive their primitive machinery but they were still among the poorest of classes; the steel that they worked was normally obtained on credit and several cutlers would have shared or rented a grinding wheel.

Later Stuart knives showing point variation, some blades with a choil (arrowed) as opposed to those with dropped edges; button bolsters predominate.

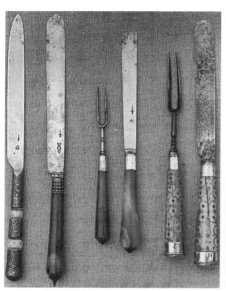

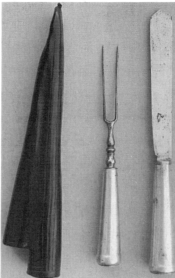

Left: *Knife and fork with plain silver cartridge hafts, each engraved with a crest on the base (detail below).*

Above: *Dagger-marked knives by London cutlers: (left to right) John Almond c.1620; William Boswell or Thomas Elliot c.1670; a knife bearing an illegible mark c.1660 with its matching fork; a knife and fork with ivory piqué hafts by Paul Browne c.1680. Note the variation in the shape of the knife points.*

By 1554 the Sheffield cutlers were governed by the sixth Earl of Shrewsbury. William Elles applied to the manor court and was granted a cutler's mark on payment of an annual rent of 1d. This was the first record of a Sheffield cutler's mark to have survived; other marks may have been granted before this. In 1565 the Sheffield cutlers were granted their first regulations, by authority of the Earl, allowing them to take on apprentices for a period of seven years. In 1590 there was a second ordinance, a quality-control law, limiting cutlers to work in that trade only, and controlling the undisciplined use of marks. The first fines of 6s 8d were issued and were paid directly to the Earl's own purse. In 1614 a still-extant register of marks was started and in 1624 the Sheffield cutlers were at last granted a charter by Parliament. The company was called the Company of Cutlers in Hallamshire.

Sheffield cutlers' marks book of 1614 showing page 8 with the name of Robert Wilkinson at the top. (Courtesy of the Cutlers' Company in Hallamshire.)

18

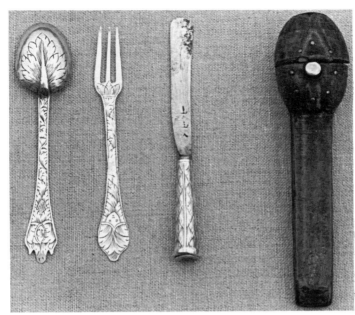

LATE STUART AND EARLY GEORGIAN (1650–1800)

During the Commonwealth, knife points, like religious images, were out of fashion. Apparently a cardinal who had witnessed the stabbing of a guest at his host's table ordered that all his household knives should have their points ground to either a right-angled or a rounded tip; this may have started a trend, since mid to late seventeenth-century knife tips diversified into triangular, square, spatulate and sloped. At the end of the century knife blades swept out into a curved scimitar, a style that continued throughout most of the eighteenth century. Blades with edges directly in line with the bolster were made with a choil whereas new-style blades, with the edge lower than the bolster, appeared *c.*1760-70 and did not require a choil. Blades with dropped edges were slightly more versatile, many were made into utility knives for the kitchen or the poorer classes and were often scale-tanged and made with a short octagonal or cylindrical bolster.

The Restoration of the monarchy in 1660 revived some of the pre-Commonwealth splendour and introduced a new-style spoon and table fork from France.

The style was known as *pied de biche* as the three-lobed end bears a resemblance to a doe's foot, but it is more commonly known as *trefid.* At first these were sold singly, in pairs or in sets of six; during the 1680s sets of trefid spoons with matching knives and even table forks (at last) suggest that guests were often being supplied with table cutlery. The more affluent classes afforded sets of knives and other tableware still incorporating basic Commonwealth and Restoration designs but which were enriched with superb engraving and made in a greater variety of materials. Providing a place setting of knife, fork perhaps and spoon became *de rigueur.* It was not, however, until the turn of the century, with the evolution of the 'dognose' pattern (*c.*1695-1720), that sets of flatware (non-ferrous forks and spoons), as opposed to cutlery (ferrous-bladed knives and forks), were laid together as the first full place settings at the dining tables of the more affluent. As the distinction between courses at a meal became more socially acceptable so did table cutlery and flatware begin to be subdivided by size into table knives, table spoons, table forks and smaller cheese knives, dessert spoons and forks.

It was still advisable to carry a personal knife, however, since not all hosts were wealthy and if a guest came without a knife or spoon he might well have to eat with his fingers. In his 1663 diary Pepys complained that a Guildhall supper, to which he had been invited, was laid with knives only at the two top tables. Fortunately he had just purchased a fine 'aggate-hafted knife' from Pope's Alley close by Cornhill, where many cutlers' shops were situated. A diner who disliked sullying his hands would use the knife's point to convey food. A bowl and ewer of water were sometimes provided to rinse sticky fingers (Emmerson, 1991). During the seventeenth century, eating habits slowly evolved towards using a knife and fork together. Forks were slow to catch on: the English disliked this foreign habit but by the time of King George I had grown accustomed to using them. From eating in the large and draughty hall, families moved to a room specifically designed for dining. Travellers required folding cutlery and many

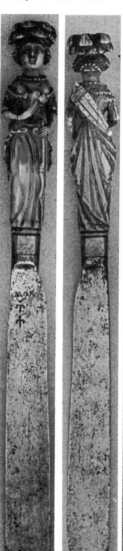

The front and back of seventeenth-century knives with carved ivory hafts depicting classical figures: Jupiter, Diana, Bacchus and a soldier.

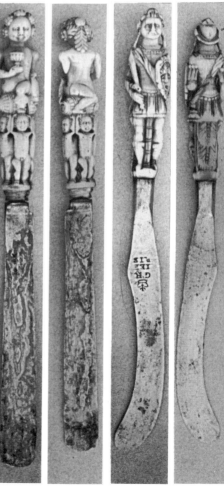

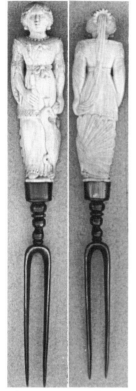

The front and back of a seventeenth-century fork depicting the classical figure of Juno.

Still life by Peter Claesz (1635), with a seventeenth-century knife as a standard part of the composition. (Courtesy of Koninklijk Museum voor Schone Kunsten, Antwerp.)

Knife with bone haft, c.1680, carved by its owner, Daniel Cleark, in 1682, with 'She that I lend this I vove [vow] to kis'.

DANIEL CLEARK
HIS KNIFE SHE THAT
I LEND THAIS I VOVE TO
KIS DE THE 19 1682

pieces were made conveniently smaller, or with threaded tangs and hafts, so that they could be unscrewed and collapsed into pocket-sized containers.

Boxes were made to hold sets of knives, forks and spoons. These were crudely made from wood and then smartened up with leather or shagreen veneer. The lids were hinged and slope-fronted whilst the interiors, lined with plush velvet and wire braid, normally held a dozen knives and forks and half a dozen spoons. By the 1780s these were being made in the same style but veneered in mahogany and inlaid with marquetry shells and stars in keeping with the Sheraton style of furniture from that period. By the end of the century larger sets of table cutlery were kept in neo-classical wooden urns that could hold 120 knives and forks.

During the reign of William and Mary many Dutch knives with beautifully carved ivory hafts were imported. Not to be outdone, the English cutlers responded by reviving and improving their own haft-carving techniques, although many may have resorted to importing such hafts from centres of carving excellence such as Dieppe.

The blades of some knives were interestingly engraved with 'cutlers' poetry',

21

> *My Love is fixt I will not range,*
> *I like my choice I will not change* — Elizabeth Walles
>
> *Witt wealth and Beauty, all doe well*
> *But Constant Love doth farr excell,* — Elizabeth Walles 1676

Pair of knives that belonged to Elizabeth Walles and engraved with couplets along the blades: 'My love is fixt, I will not range – I like my choice, I will not change' and 'Witt, wealth and Beauty, all doe well – But Constant Love doth farr excell. Elizabeth Walles – 1676.'

a charming idea started during the reign of Charles II, when the fashion for giving rings engraved with lovers' short posies was popular. Many couplets warn the user of the sharpness of the blade or bear a more romantic inscription. Knife ownership was still important and one, dated 1682, belonged to a certain Daniel Cleark, who himself may have carved the haft with its charming couplet.

Until about 1740, bolsters for knife blades were often cylindrical or comprised a ball and disc incorporating a deep choil. The bolster was shortened to a simple cap about 1770. A scimitar-bladed knife was made with an upturned spatulate tip that also doubled as a spoon since fork tines were often made of steel and of these some were still needle-sharp. A French diarist noted in 1799: 'I am not much disposed to risk pricking my mouth or tongue with those little sharp steel tridents which are generally used even in the best houses of England.' He continued to describe how forks were used to hold food down whilst being cut up. The sharp fork tines scratched the pewter or tin-glazed Delft plates on which they were used. Silver fork tines also suffered, becoming nicked by sharp steel knife blades. Silver forks are consequently rarer than spoons. This has led to the conversion of eighteenth-century spoons into forks and this collector's pitfall is carefully explained in Pickford (1983).

Steel-bladed knives and forks were often made with a hollow silver haft for the insertion of remeltable resin and ash to hold the tang fast. Since silver is possibly the best conductor of heat, a prolonged immersion of any resin-loaded silver haft in hot water causes the resin to soften and the blade to rise. The resin has always been tightly packed into the haft to prevent damage should the knife be dropped – the silver surface would dent only slightly. At the end of the seventeenth century hafts were normally cylinder-shaped, like a cannon, but a few curved downwards like a pistol grip to match the upturned tilt of the knife point. During the early 1720s the pistol grip became the standard design for knife hafts. The sharply pointed, steel-bladed forks were hafted in like manner although

Later eighteenth-century knives and forks, including one hafted in green-stained ivory (one from bottom), with scrolling or truncated ends c.1770–90.

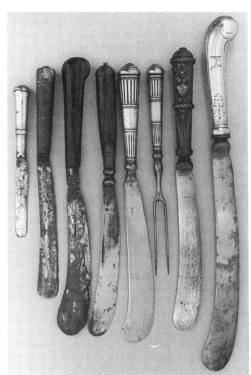

Late seventeenth/early eighteenth-century knives and a fork with cannon-shaped hafts. Note that scimitar blades from this period lack a hump to the back.

Porcelain tableware, which arrived in England from the Orient during the seventeenth century, was largely confined to plates and cups. As its versatility was realised it was used as a hafting material and many eighteenth-century knives and forks (and a few spoons) were hafted with either earthenware or porcelain. The demand for ceramic handles prompted imports from many European factories, particularly Meissen, St Cloud, Chantilly and Villeroy. The English factories at Chelsea, Bow and Worcester quickly stepped in. Their soft-paste hafts were rather restrained in taste compared with those from the continent but were evidently popular.

Most English porcelain hafts were made for 'knock-on' tanged blades and had a fairly wide channel to accommodate both the tang and the resin-based filler. The channel through a continental haft was narrower and pierced at the other end for a 'through tang', capped with a metal pommel or disc rather in the style of later sixteenth-century knives. In either case the top end of a haft was almost always protected by a metal ferrule which also served to conceal any unsightly firing marks.

Ceramic hafts were made in moulds, often plain or faceted; some incorporated a raised design which novice collectors

with slightly smaller hafts. At the table the full set of cutlery became more commonplace and would have included a table spoon for drinking soup, with the table fork either accompanying the table spoon to help eat any solid morsels in the soup or used to convey meat courses to the mouth. Steel-bladed dessert knives and forks were used for cutting cheese and cakes, and both (flatware) dessert spoons and forks were confined to eating softer foodstuffs such as lemon jelly, chocolate cream or even frumenty (wheat porridge), which had been a popular accompaniment to venison since the fifteenth century.

Later seventeenth-century steel-bladed forks.

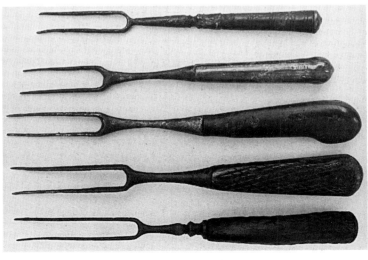

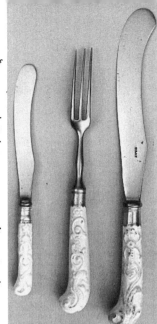

Left: *Differentiation of solid silver flatware (left) as opposed to steel-bladed cutlery, c.1750: note that the silver forks were three-tined whereas those in steel still had only two. Ownership marks can be seen on the silver items, including the chough of the Ithell family (centre dessert knife).*

Right: *Porcelain hafts: Worcester 'snake' on creamware hafts c.1745–60: (from left) St Cloud, c.1745; Worcester, c.1755–60; Bow, c.1756–8 with retailer's mark of GRAY of Eastcheap.*

may consider specific to a certain factory. However, these mouldings were copied from Chinese or French designs and were used by many English factories. Bow dominated the English market in numbers of ceramic hafts produced, and the majority were painted in underglaze blue similar to St Cloud; Bow was also renowned for its plain white hafts of mass-produced creamware with raised designs, characterised by their particular paste and glaze which did not wear well. Bow also produced polychrome handles although these are now rare. White Worcester raised-pattern hafts are known in two designs. One of these shows trailing flowers and leaves; the other incorporates a characteristic 'snake-like' squiggle in the middle of the haft which was taken from a popular baroque design of St Cloud, *c.*1733; this was also imitated by Bow.

Although it produced some rare polychrome hafts, Worcester was principally renowned for its blue and white porcelain; its finest hafts were made there during the latter part of what is known as the First Period (*c.*1758–65).

Other English factories such as New Hall made hard-paste hafts with transfer decoration in blue. The Whieldon and Wedg-wood factories produced both marbled ware and solid 'agate ware' hafts in blue-green or surface-decorated brown. Knife and fork hafts of enamel, although relatively uncommon, were produced largely on the continent, especially in Germany and France. A few English examples were made, attributed to Staffordshire *c.*1765.

Knives and forks with ceramic or enamel hafts suffered accidental abuse and many show signs of damage. This may account for their gradual decline during the early nineteenth century as people tired of their fragility and reverted once more to silver- and ivory-hafted knives and forks. Ceramic hafts have been reproduced and faked. Although fakes are comparatively rare, collectors should beware and examine differences in paste, colour and glaze.

The pistol handle was gradually phased out in the 1770s, giving way to flat-ended or diagonally truncated hafts, often made from green-stained ivory, a commonly used hafting material at this time. Shell, scroll-ended or fish-shaped hafts, made from thin sheet silver to match the feather-edged and bright-cut flatware, also appeared at this time. The knife edge became straighter and dropped away sharply at the bolster, forming a right angle and obviating the choil.

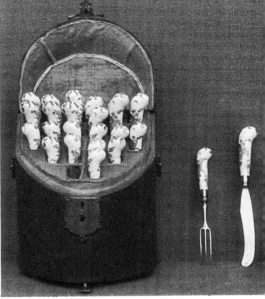

By 1770 English cutlers were steering away from French designs, perhaps deterred by anti-French feeling as Bonaparte began his conquest of Europe. This was particularly noticeable in Sheffield, where, with the opening of the assay office in 1773, the cutlers, silversmiths and platers often dabbled in each other's trades or worked hand in hand providing one another with the constituent parts of items such as folding fruit knives.

The Sheffield Cutlers' Company flourished as new mills opened along local rivers. Inventive cutlers patented new processes and blade types to suit new purposes (such as sharpening pencils) during the eighteenth century. The allied trades of silversmithing and silver fusion-plating (making Sheffield plate) were used for making the handles of table knives and the town trebled in size as new factories and shops opened. At last Sheffield was gaining both respect for its products and the upper hand over its London rivals. The Cutlers' Company in Hallamshire, as it is still known, developed its own subsidiary crafts not unlike the 'mysteries' of the London company: grinders, shearsmiths, scythesmiths, scissorsmiths, filesmiths and makers of farm and garden tools, each of whom set up or shared in the use of the metal-processing mills. Parts of the five Sheffield rivers were carefully sluiced to provide water power for driving machinery such as tilt hammers, essential to the hardening of the steel so that it produced good-quality cutlery blades that were capable of retaining a sharp edge.

The art of grinding blades was one of the cutler's less pleasant duties. The necessity for fine grinding caused the formation of a full-time subsidiary craft of grinders in the eighteenth century. A grinder either sat astride or lay down on a wooden 'horsing' to hold the blade at a steady angle as the wheel was turned by foot or hand (as in medieval times) or by water power. The grinders' trade was lowly and many did not survive the long hours of inhaling the grinding dust.

Two feather-edged knives (table and dessert/cheese) with a dessert spoon (top); two early nineteenth-century table knives and (below) two late eighteenth-century table knives.

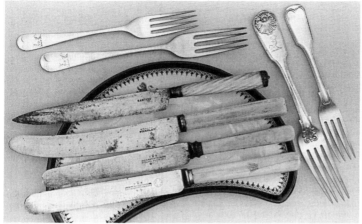

THE NINETEENTH CENTURY

The rapid advance of mechanisation swept away the already diminishing variety of knife, fork and spoon styles, replacing it with a standardisation of design. Carefully hand-constructed pieces became fewer as demand for quantity and functional quality was met by increased output from machines.

Forks were invariably four-tined and the handles turned up at the end so that they were more comfortable to hold. A steel cutting edge was added to the edge of some fork blades to be used by handicapped or one-handed persons. One celebrated silver-gilt example belonged to Lord Nelson.

By 1800 the scimitar blade had been superseded by the spear-pointed blade and the broad, straight, parallel-sided and round-tipped blade with the dropped edge, which latterly became the standard pattern for the nineteenth and much of the earlier twentieth centuries.

The bolster was short, normally oval in cross-section, sometimes polymorphic, although basically simple; it was forged on to the cutting part of the blade as in previous centuries. Although the scale tang was generally used for 'lower-class' or kitchen cutlery, the narrow-pointed whittle tang predominated. By the mid century it was gradually superseded by the pin tang, which was more uniform, comprising a narrow cylindrical shaft. However neat this may have appeared and however easy it was to drill the haft for its insertion, this innovation unfortunately reduced the knife's efficiency. The bolster still needed to be capable of sustaining a force greater than that of the downward cutting stroke and many tangs were bent and hafts split if the knife was used with undue force. This may have been a ruse of the cutlers to build in obsolescence and gain more trade.

Hafting materials remained unchanged and were dominated by silver and ivory, often stained green. Bone, horn and wood were still used to haft utility knives. European porcelain and agate, often stained, were still favoured throughout most of the century but were mainly reserved for decorative dessert knives and forks. The art of the pearler came into its greatest demand at this time, giving rise to hafts of mother-of-pearl either engraved with period motifs or skilfully carved with the most elaborate and imaginative designs. With the increase in the range of tableware, such as tea cutlery and, later (c.1880), fish knives and forks, mother-of-pearl was found to be as attractive as ivory and cheaper. It did not split in dry weather and better-quality nacre showed a diversity of colour; those makers who were wary of its fragility protected it with gilt metal caps.

Making good-quality steel was a lengthy process but the invention of the Bessemer converter in 1856, which could produce large quantities of mild carbon steel for knife and tool blades, led to the mass-production of cutlery during the latter half of the nineteenth century. The process largely outmoded the more labour-intensive method of producing steel in fireclay crucibles.

Surrounded by the expanding steel industry, the Sheffield cutlers eclipsed those of London. Two particular firms, George Wostenholm and Joseph Rodgers, were daily producing masses of top-quality cutlery. Throughout the British Empire the name of Rodgers became a byword for quality. The names of many Sheffield cutlery firms are still recognised today by their marks either stamped or etched on to blades, even though most of the firms have since disappeared. Many companies made blades for retailers all over Britain who stamped their names and addresses on to the wares although the blades were almost invariably made at Sheffield. Occasionally a retailer's name occurs combined with a Sheffield cutler's device and even more occasionally knives are found bearing marks of some other provincial cutlers' company, such as Salisbury.

Knives bladed with carbon steel were still found to taint certain foodstuffs and, for those who could afford it, blades were close-plated with silver, an ancient process that had been revived since c.1780. Medieval-style banquets became popular in the nineteenth century and tables were laid, according to rules set down by Mrs Isabella Beeton and many other writers on Victorian housewifery, with large services of table cutlery and flatware. Silvered blades had to be cleaned and those blades that were unplated were particularly difficult. After the feast, the washing up would have been daunting, as so many other pieces of tableware had been devised since medieval times, when guests conveniently took their knives away with them. Knife cleaners were invented to remove the black stain from the carbon steel blades and, although this reduced the drudgery, it ultimately led to the blades wearing out more quickly because the circular brush applied cleaning grit with added vigour.

The renaissance of the medieval-style banquet necessitated many place settings, perhaps as many as fifty or sixty. Cutlery urns were gradually phased out in favour of less decorative but functional canteens of cutlery, produced so that large households could cater for so many guests. Even a single place-setting could be laid with up to ten pieces of cutlery and flatware, including the newly invented and round-bowled soup spoon which appeared on tables around 1900. The displaced table spoon, in turn, became a serving spoon. Other serving pieces of flatware became more specialised and could only be used for serving certain types of food such as fish. Knives and forks specifically designed for eating fish date back to the mid nineteenth century but were thought by many to be rather middle-class; Queen Victoria ate fish using two forks, a regal habit that persists to this day.

Fork-cum-knife with an applied steel edge for a one-handed person; this example belonged to Lord Nelson. (Courtesy of Terry Atkins, Nelson Museum at Lloyds of London.)

ARTS AND CRAFTS TO THE PRESENT

Stainless steel was discovered and developed at Sheffield early in the twentieth century by Harry Brearley of Thomas Firth & Sons and in 1914 the first stainless steel knife blades were forged, revolutionising the cutlery industry. Stainless steel was not confined to a knife's blade and tang but was also used to form the haft. Apart from a post-war revival, stainless steel largely replaced the fruit knife's less durable blade of silver. By the end of the 1920s fruit and other dessert knives were rarely made from silver and since stainless steel was harder to decorate knife blades became plainer. Plastics such as bakelite, ivorine and xylo were used for making knife hafts, as were plastic hardstones imitating agate. The man-made materials were considerably easier to work as well as being cheaper.

However, sophisticated technology enabled knives, forks and spoons made of stainless steel to be produced in imaginative designs. Spoons especially, and other tableware, were popular subjects for the art and craft movements that started in the 1880s: the bold colours and flowing lines of Art Nouveau and, later, the angular Art Deco designs. Designers such as C. R. Ashbee (c.1900), Omar Ramsden and Alwyn Carr (c.1900–30), W. H. Haseler (c.1900), C. R. Mackintosh (c.1900) and the Keswick School of Industrial Arts produced silver flatware and a few knives of Celtic or primitive form enhanced with brightly coloured enamel or other decoration. In the early part of the twentieth century Liberty commissioned designs by Archibald Knox for their pewter Tudric and silver Cymric wares. Treasured by their owners, they are now highly collectable. Christopher Dresser (c.1870–90), a break-away designer of the later nineteenth century, produced plain and ergonomic designs for the tableware market and designed some flatware,

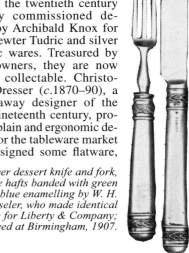

Knife with stainless steel blade and electro-plated fork, c.1920.

Silver dessert knife and fork, the hafts banded with green and blue enamelling by W. H. Haseler, who made identical pieces for Liberty & Company; assayed at Birmingham, 1907.

Silver Arrow pattern flatware by Stuart Devlin, c.1980. (Courtesy of Stuart Devlin & Company.)

although this is rarely encountered.

The Danish firm of George Jensen continued this trend, particularly in the 1920s and 1930s, producing some superb examples of flatware including the 'Kaktus' pattern, which has now become universally associated with that firm.

Since then designers such as Charles Boyton (1950s) and his French counterpart Jean Puiforcat (1920s and 1930s), who studied in London, have continued and yet mellowed the Dresser-style severity and have inspired others with their table cutlery, plain yet with stepped ends or flowing lines. Although the convenience and cheapness of the age of plastic has struck a severe blow, trend-setting silversmiths who are members of the London Goldsmiths' Company still produce many eye-catching pieces and in this designer-conscious age we may once again become more aware of our heritage in table cutlery.

FURTHER READING

Amme, J. *Historic Cutlery*. Arnoldsche, Stuttgart, 2002.

Bailey, C.T.P. *Knives and Forks*. Medici Society, 1927.

Benker, G. *Alte Bestecke*. Callwey, Munich, 1978.

Boggiali, G. *La Posata*. Milla Editrice, Milan, 1987.

Brown, W. H. (Bill). 'Eating Implements', *Antique Collecting* 29 (9), 21-23, 1995.

Brown, W. H. (Bill) *et al. British Cutlery – An Illustrated History of Design, Evolution and Use* (editor P. Brown). Philip Wilson Publishers, London, 2001.

Cowgill, J., de Neergard, M., and Griffiths, N. *Knives and Scabbards*. HMSO (Museum of London), 1987.

De Riaz, Y. *Le livre des couteaux* ('The Book of Knives'). Edita, Lausanne, 1978.

Frederiks, J.W. 'Gegraveerde Gotische Mesheften', *Nederlandsch Kunsthistorisch Jaarboek*, 217–37, 1947.

Hammond, P.W. *Food and Feast in Mediaeval England*. Alan Sutton (UK) and Dover (USA), 1993.

Hayward, J.F. *English Cutlery, 16th to 18th Century*. HMSO, 1957.

Himsworth, J.B. *The Story of Cutlery, from Flint to Stainless Steel*. Ernest Benn, 1953.

Hughes, G.B. 'Evolution of the Silver Table Fork', *Country Life* 127, 364–5, 1959.

Lassen, E. *Knives, Forks and Spoons*. Høst & Søn, Copenhagen, 1960.

Levine, E. *Levine's Guide to Knives and Their Values*. DBI Books Inc, Northbrook, Illinois, 1985; second edition 1989; third edition 1993.

Moore, S.J. 'English Table Cutlery', *Antique Dealer and Collectors' Guide*, May 1979, 64–8, and June 1979, 67–9.

Moore, S.J. 'Pocket Knives at Table? Whatever Next', *Petits Propos Culinaires* 16, 35–41. Prospect Books, 1984.

Moore, S.J. *Penknives and Other Folding Knives*. Shire, 1988; reprinted 2006.

Moore, S.J. 'Collecting Inscribed Flatware and Knives', *Antique Collecting* 25 (2), 29–34, 1990.

Moore, S.J. 'Carvers and Carving Knives', *The National Knife Magazine* 18, (11), 28-30, Chattanooga, Tennessee, 1995.

Moore, S.J. *Cutlery for the Table – A History of British Table and Pocket Cutlery*. The Hallamshire Press Ltd, Sheffield, 1999.

Paston-Williams, S. *A History of Cooking and Eating*. National Trust, 1993.

Pearce, M. 'Neglected Cutlery', *Antique Collecting* 14 (2), 20–22, 1979.

Singleton, H.R. *A Chronology of Cutlery*. Sheffield City Museums, 1973.

Smithurst, P. *The Cutlery Industry*. Shire, 1987.

Tweedale, G. *Giants of Sheffield Steel*. Sheffield City Libraries, 1986.

Victoria and Albert Museum. *Masterpieces of Cutlery and the Art of Eating* (exhibition catalogue). Victoria and Albert Museum, 1979.

Welch, C. *History of the Cutlers' Company of London and of the Minor Cutlery Crafts with Biographical Notices of Early London Cutlers*. Cutlers' Company, London, 1916, 1923.

REFERENCES

Anonymous. *The Boke of Kervynge*. Printed by Wynkyn de Worde, London, 1506 and 1513.

Blair, C. 'The London Cutlers' Dagger Mark', note on the menu of the Stewards' Dinner, Worshipful Company of Cutlers of London, 1987.

Emmerson, R. *Table Settings*. Shire, 1991.

Hey, D. *The Fiery Blades of Hallamshire*. Leicester University Press, 1991.

Leader, R.E. *History of the Company of Cutlers in Hallamshire in the County of York*, volumes I-II. Sheffield, 1959.

Moore, S.J. *Spoons 1650-2000*. Shire, 1987; second edition 2005.

Pickford, I. *Silver Flatware*. Antique Collectors' Club, Woodbridge, 1983.

PLACES TO VISIT

GREAT BRITAIN

The British Museum, Great Russell Street, London WC1B 3DG. Telephone: 020 7323 8000. Website: www.british-museum.ac.uk Exceptional collection of prehistoric, ancient civilisation and Anglo-Saxon weapon cutlery.

The Company of Cutlers in Hallamshire, Cutlers' Hall, Church Street, Sheffield, South Yorkshire S1 1HG. Telephone: 0114 272 8456. Website: www.cutlers-hallamshire.org.uk By appointment. Collection of Sheffield cutlery from mid seventeenth century onwards; some exceptional pieces.

Fitzwilliam Museum, Trumpington Street, Cambridge CB2 1RB. Telephone: 01223 332900. Website: www.fitzmuseum.cam.ac.uk Small but notable collection of post-medieval European cutlery.

Kelham Island Museum (part of Sheffield Industrial Museums Trust), Alma Street, off Corporation Street, Sheffield, South Yorkshire S3 8RY. Telephone: 0114 272 2106. Website: www.simt.co.uk Mainly steel-processing and silver-plating industries; cutler's workbench and Sheffield mesters (working cutlers) at work.

Millennium Galleries, Arundel Gate, Sheffield, South Yorkshire S1 2PP. Telephone: 0114 278 2600. Website: www.sheffieldgalleries.org.uk Good collection and gallery devoted to eating and other cutlery. The table cutlery was augmented in 2003 by the addition of the renowned Bill Brown collection.

Museum of London, 150 London Wall, London EC2Y 5HN. Telephone: 0870 444 3852. Website: www.museumoflondon.org.uk Broad collection of mainly London-excavated material since prehistory.

Salisbury and South Wiltshire Museum, The King's House, 65 The Close, Salisbury, Wiltshire SP1 2EN. Telephone: 01722 332151. Website: www.salisburymuseum.org.uk Small collection of cutlery, some unusual pieces.

Victoria and Albert Museum, Cromwell Road, South Kensington, London SW7 2RL. Telephone: 020 7942 2000. Website: www.vam.ac.uk Several cases of post-medieval British and European cutlery; the 'Monarch Set' is in the Primary Galleries.

Worshipful Company of Cutlers, Cutlers' Hall, Warwick Lane, London EC4M 7BR. Telephone: 020 7248 1866. Website: www.cutlerslondon.co.uk By appointment. Fine collection of medieval and later British and European cutlery.

FRANCE

Musée de Cluny, 6 Place Paul-Painlevé, F-75005 Paris. Website: www.musee-moyenage.fr

Musée de la Coutellerie, Espace Pelletier, Place Charles de Gaulle, F-52800 Nogent-en-Bassigny.

Musée de la Coutellerie, Maison des Couteliers, 58 rue de la Coutellerie, F-63300 Thiers, Puy-de-Dôme. Website: www.musee-coutellerie-thiers.com Wide-ranging collection of post-medieval European and local cutlery.

Musée du Breuil Saint Germain, 2 rue Chambrulard, F-52200 Langres. An appointment is essential as the cutlery collection is presently housed in the curator's office. Fine collection of Langrois cutlery, mid seventeenth to twentieth century.

Musée du Louvre, Palais du Louvre, F-75041 Paris. Website: www.louvre.fr

GERMANY

Deutches Klingenmuseum, Klosterhof 4, 42653 Solingen, Nordrhein-Westfalen. Website: www.klingenmuseum.de Large collection of antique eating cutlery and weaponry.